IRISH MUSIC FOR GUITAR

Traditional music, song-airs and O'Carolan tunes. Music notation and guitar tab.
Pieces range from from very easy to recital standard. Recording included

arranged for
solo/classic guitar by

JOHN LOESBERG

OSSIAN

Special thanks to Ruairi O'Flaherty for tidying up the
recording and always hitting the right note.

Fingering edited by
Simon Taylor
A.L.C.M, L.L.C.M. (T.D.), F.L.C.M.

Published by
Ossian Publications

Exclusive Distributors:
Contact us:
Hal Leonard
7777 West Bluemound Road,
Milwaukee, WI 53213
Email: info@halleonard.com

In Europe, contact:
Hal Leonard Europe Limited
42 Wigmore Street, Marylebone,
London WIU 2RY
Email: info@halleonardeurope.com

In Australia, contact:
Hal Leonard Australia Pty. Ltd.
4 Lentara Court, Cheltenham,
Victoria 9132, Australia
Email: info@halleonard.com.au

Order No. OMB160
ISBN 1-900428-52-0
First published 1981
This book © Copyright 2005 Novello & Company Limited,
part of The Music Sales Group.

www.halleonard.com

From the Sean Nos - the unaccompanied style of singing from the west coast, with its Arab/Indian overtones - to the Anglo-Irish ballad tradition and the magnificent art of the Irish harpers, Ireland yields a rich harvest to those willing to undergo its musical spell.

Many forms of music dating back centuries have survived in Ireland due to its geographical position on the fringe of Europe and also because of the traditional element in cultural and other matters.

Apart from adding to the repertoire, the arranger hopes that this volume of Irish pieces will also stimulate the player's curiosity so that he or she may want to find out more about the many facets of Irish music.

The completion of this work would have been long and tortuous without the help of Simon Taylor who, as well as performing all of the pieces on the accompanying CD, found the time and energy to straighten me out on fingerings and many of the practicalities of writing for the guitar.

Thanks are also due to Douglas Gunn, an expert on Carolan's music, who himself arranged many Carolan pieces for a variety of instruments. Andrew Shiels - himself a composer and musician - expertly looked after the music-typesetting and helped out in so many other ways.

Do feel free to experiment with the music; many pieces can be played using different techniques, different emphasis and repeats may be adlibbed too, I've given guidelines, but it's up to you to make these wonderful tunes your very own !

John Loesberg
Cork, Ireland 2005

THE RIGHTS OF MAN

traditional Irish
arr. by John Loesberg

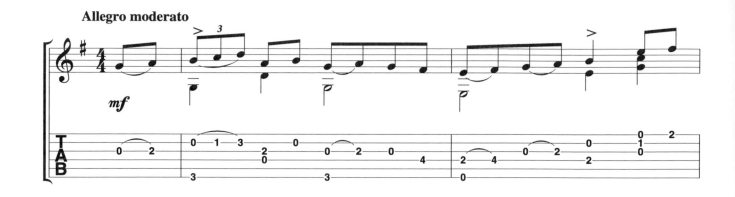

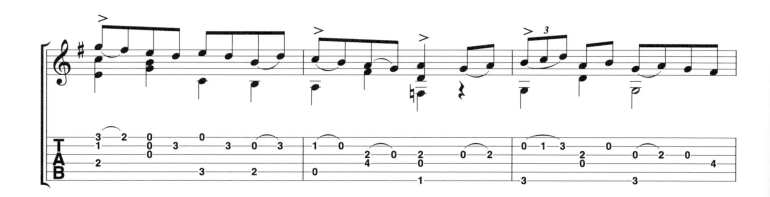

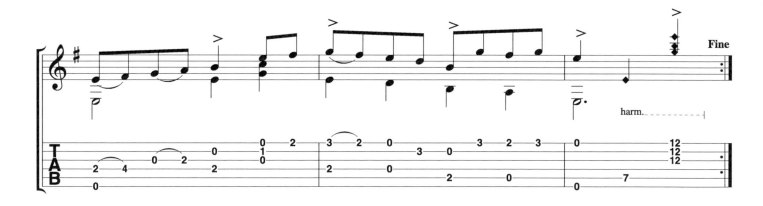

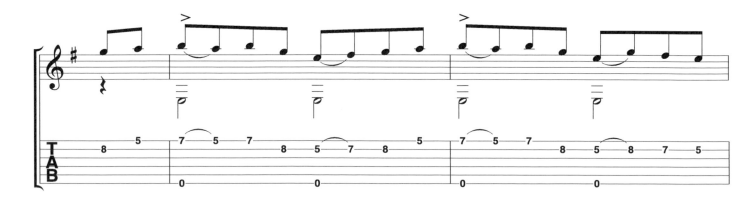

D.C. al Fine

5

THE BOYS OF BLUEHILL

traditional Irish
arr. by John Loesberg

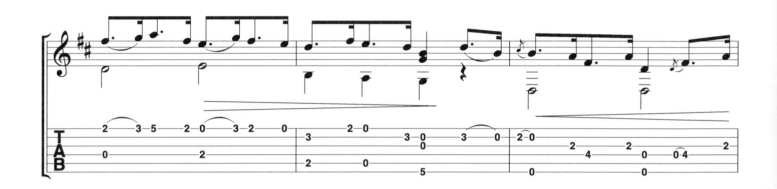

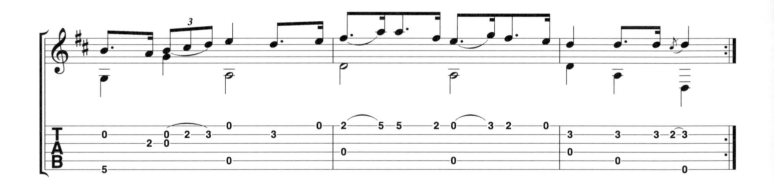

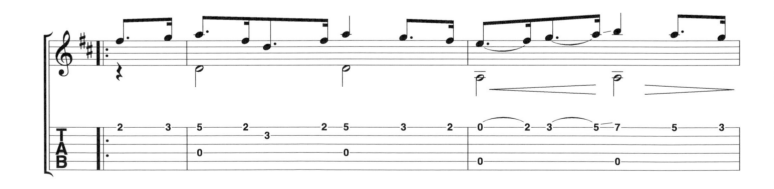

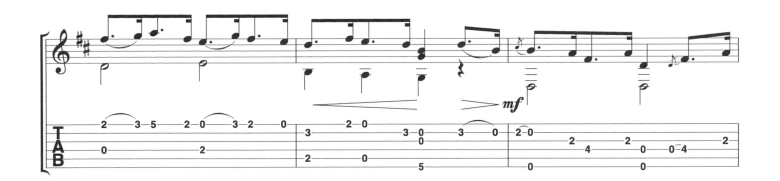

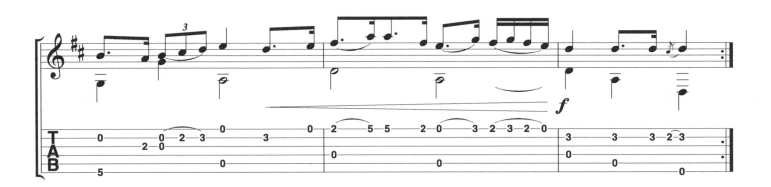

She Moved Through the Fair

traditional Irish
arr. by John Loesberg

Adagio

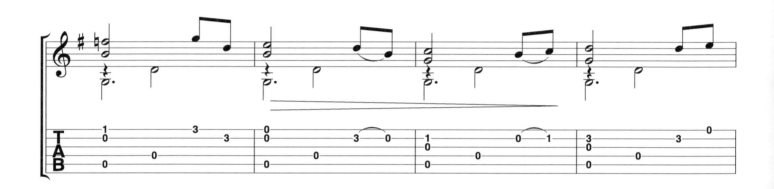

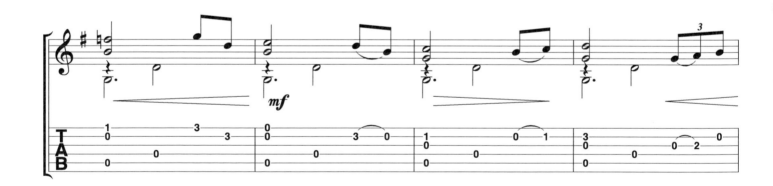

a tempo

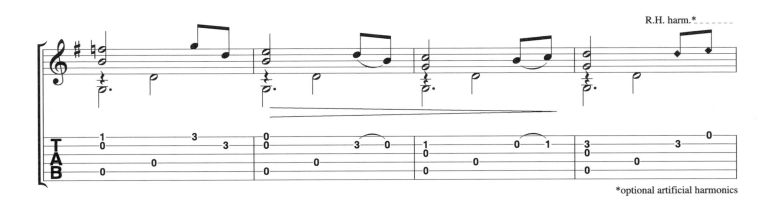

R.H. harm.*

*optional artificial harmonics

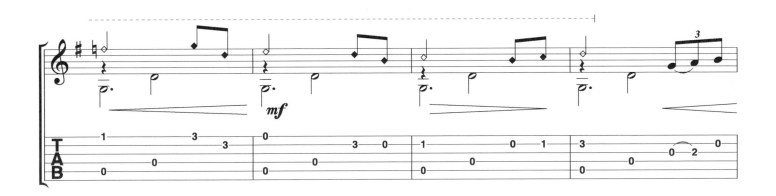

mf

molto rit.

pp

9

Báidín Pheilimí

traditional Irish
arr. by John Loesberg

11

Fear an Bháta

traditional Irish
arr. by John Loesberg

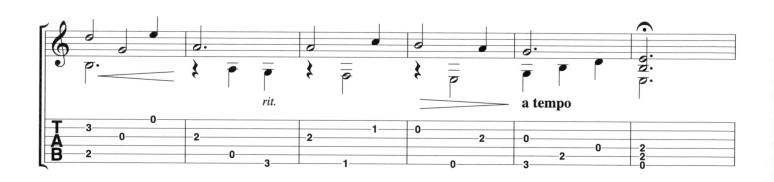

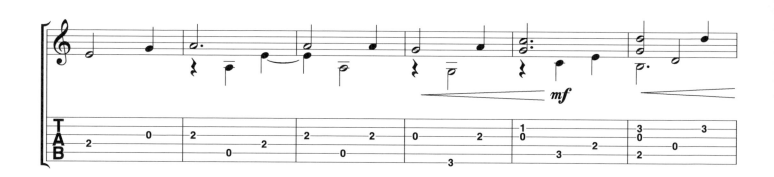

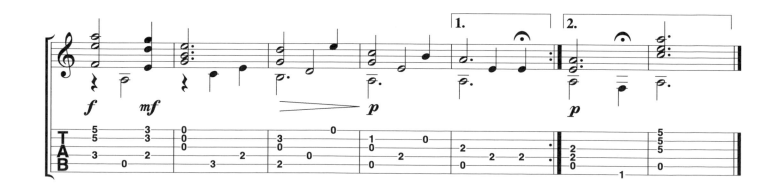

TRACK 5

The Lark in the Clear Air

traditional Irish
arr. by John Loesberg

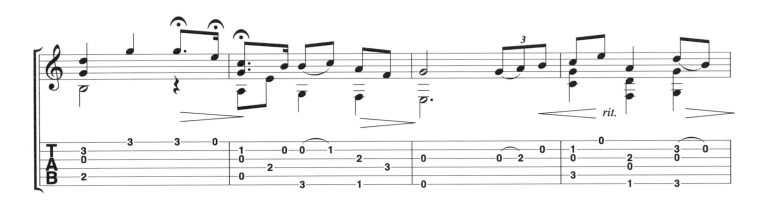

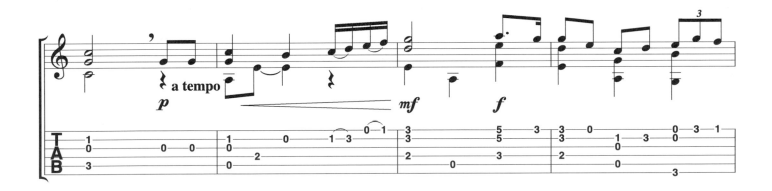

TRACK 6

Boulavogue

traditional Irish
arr. by John Loesberg

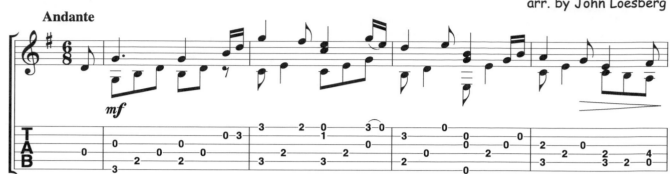

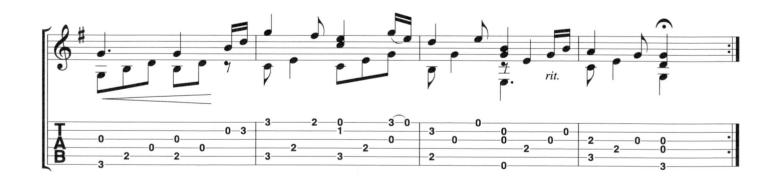

14

EILEEN AROON

Cearbhaill O'Dalaigh (14th cent.)
arr. by John Loesberg

Larghetto

TRACK 8

16

Did you see the Black Rogue

traditional Irish
arr. by John Loesberg

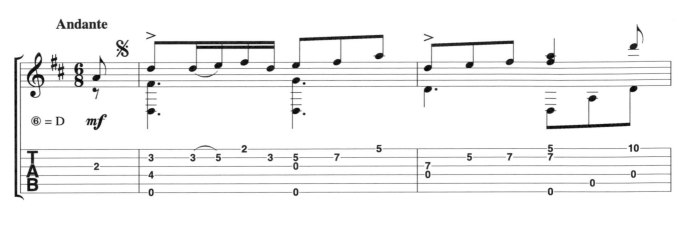

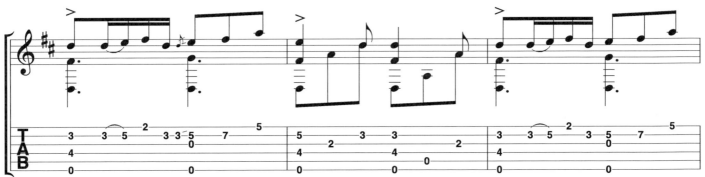

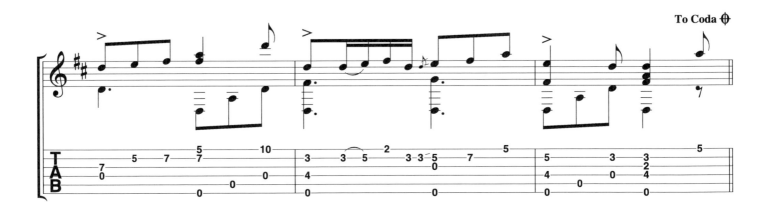

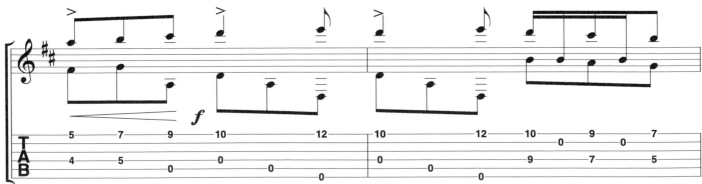

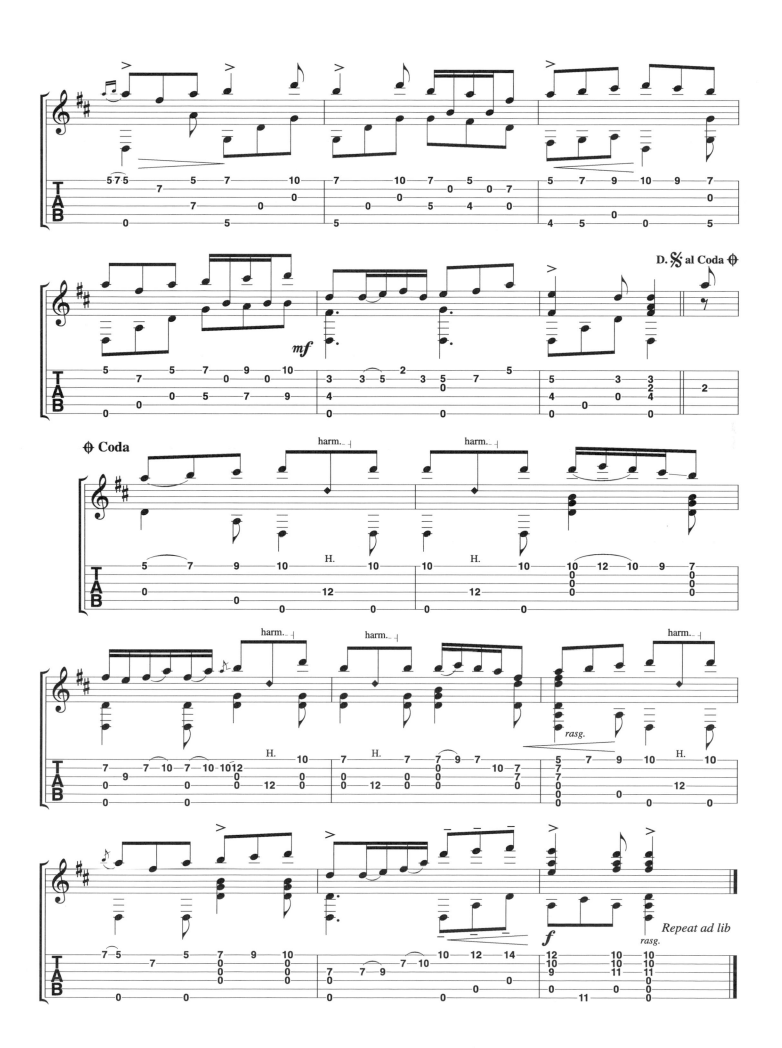

DOWN BY THE SALLY GARDENS

traditional Irish
arr. by John Loesberg

Larghetto

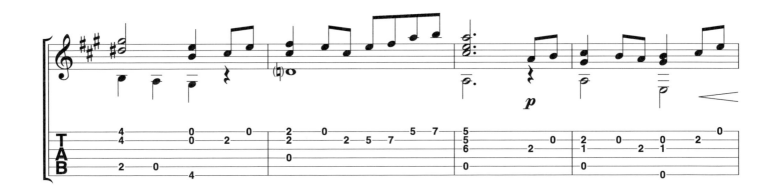

TRACK 10

THE SPINNINGWHEEL SONG

John F. Waller (1809-1894)
arr. by John Loesberg

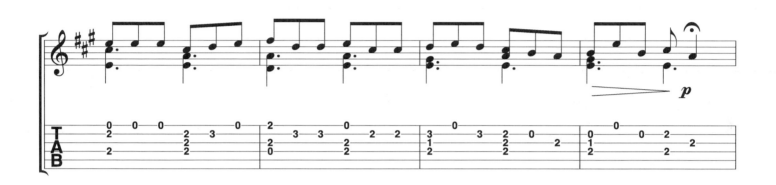

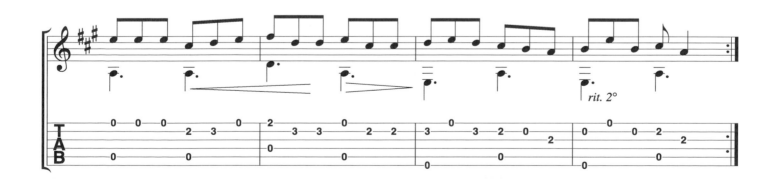

TRACK 11

SPANCIL HILL

traditional Irish
arr. by John Loesberg

Andante

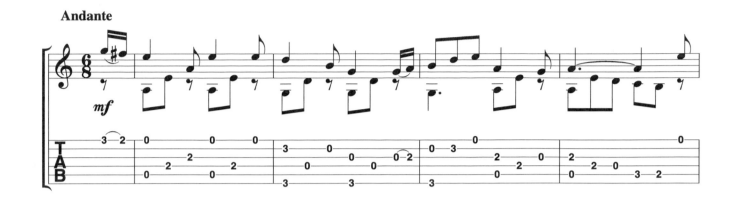

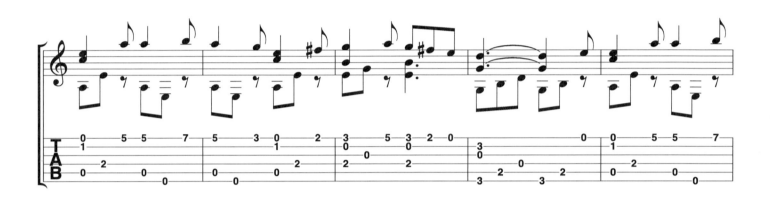

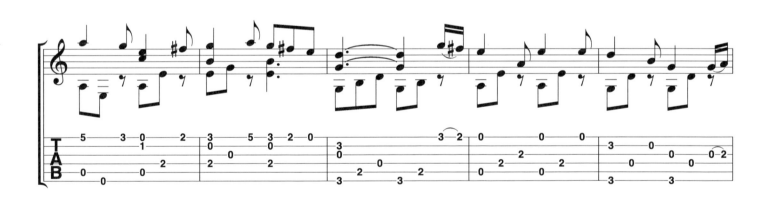

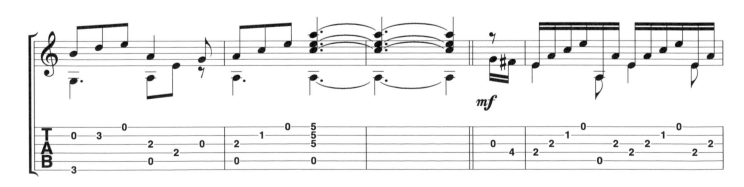

TRACK 12

CARRICKFERGUS

traditional Irish
arr. by John Loesberg

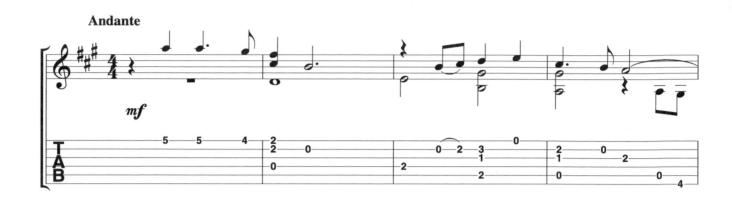

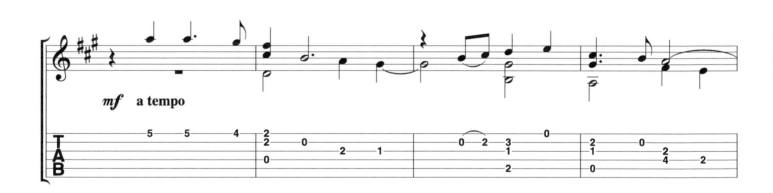

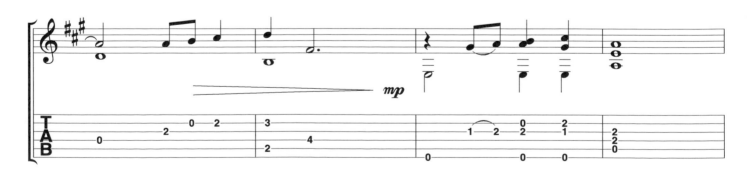

TRACK 13

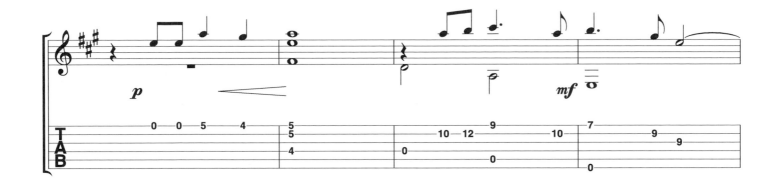

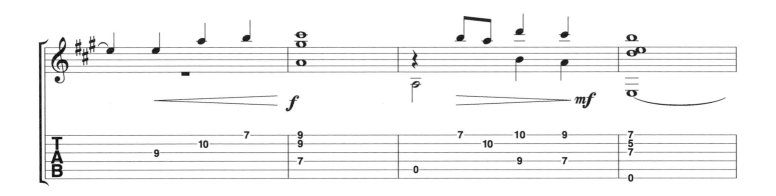

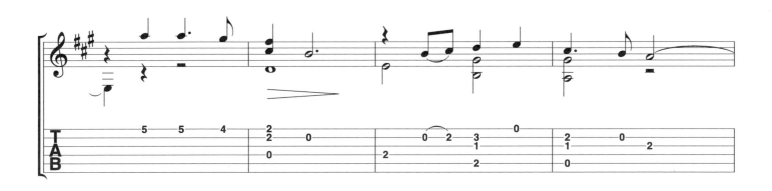

THE IRISH WASHERWOMAN

traditional Irish
arr. by John Loesberg

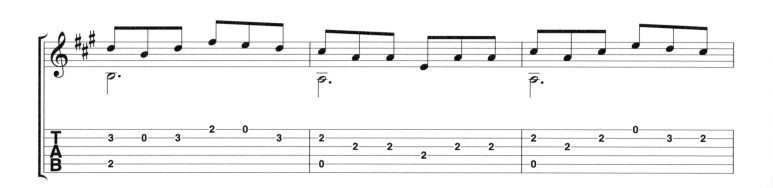

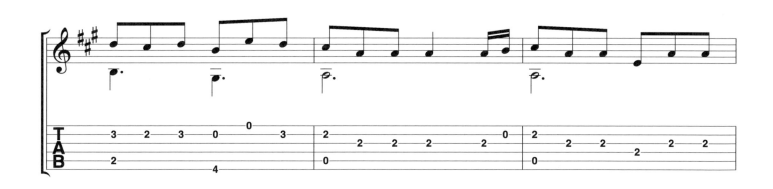

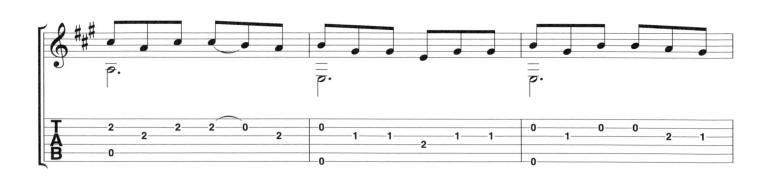

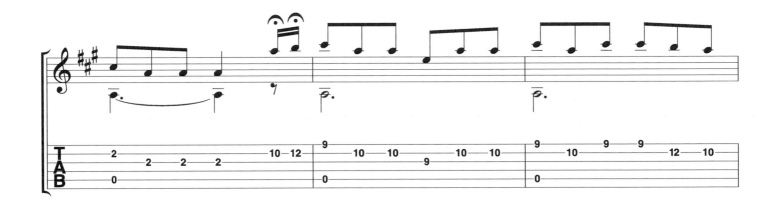

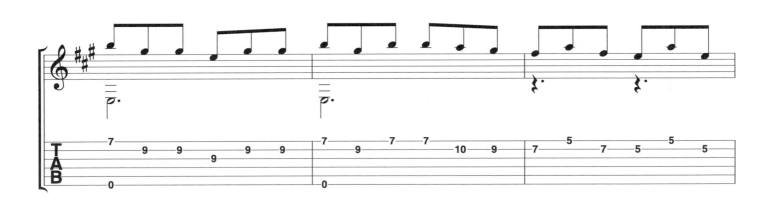

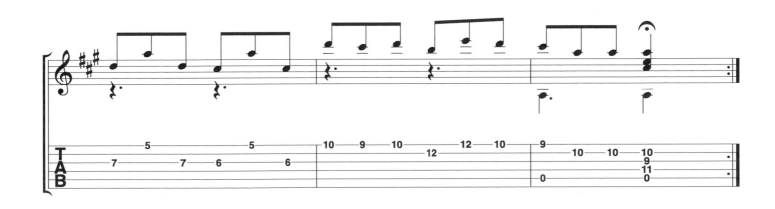

Planxty Irwin

Turlough O Carolan (1670-1738)
arr. by John Loesberg

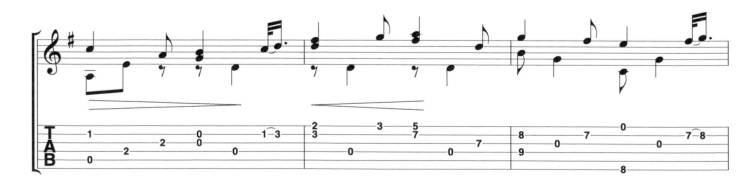

TRACK 15

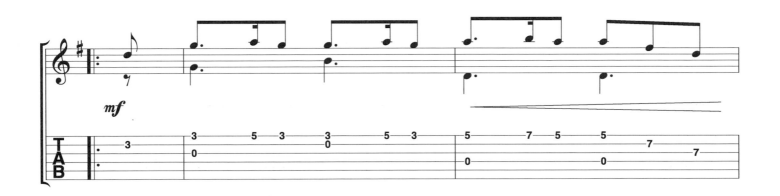

Planxty Judge

Turlough O Carolan (1670-1738)
arr. by John Loesberg

Allegro

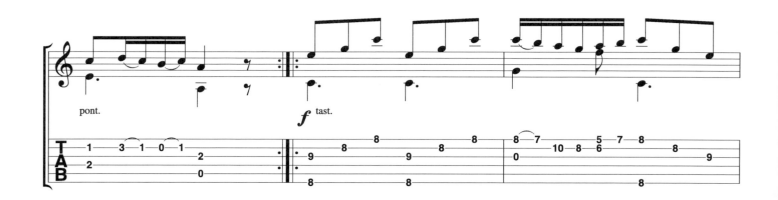

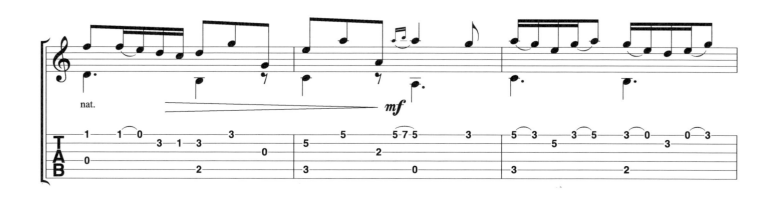

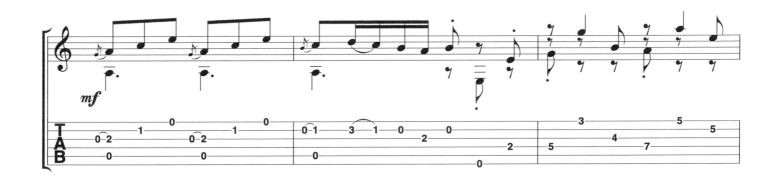

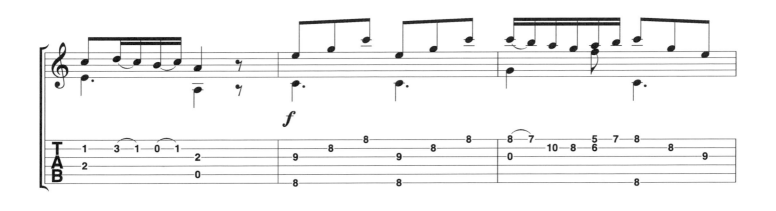

31

PLANXTY MAGUIRE

Turlough O Carolan (1670-1738)
arr. by John Loesberg

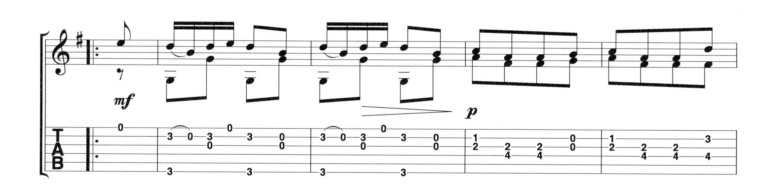

TRACK 17

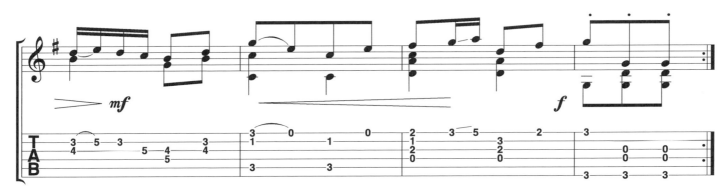

D.C. al Fine

33

THE LAMENTATION OF OWEN O'NEILL

Turlough O Carolan (1670-1738)
arr. by John Loesberg

Andante maestoso

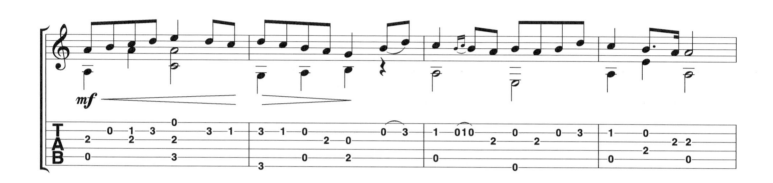

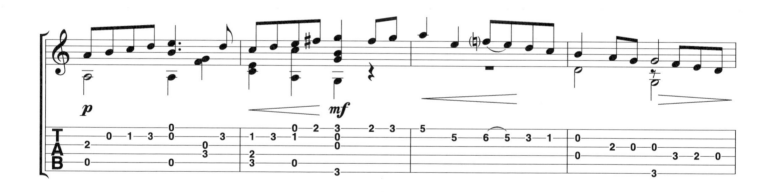

34

TRACK 18

Carolan's Concerto

Turlough O Carolan (1670-1738)
arr. by John Loesberg

TRACK
19

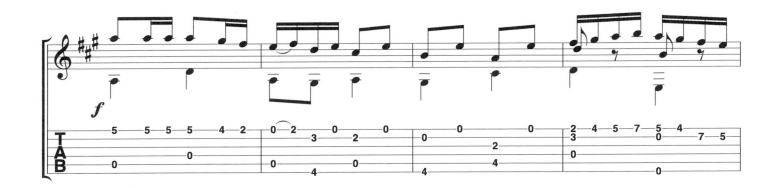

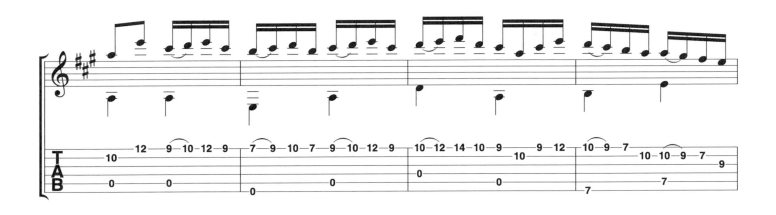

Planxty Charles Coote

Turlough O Carolan (1670-1738)
arr. by John Loesberg

Tempo di Gavotta

38

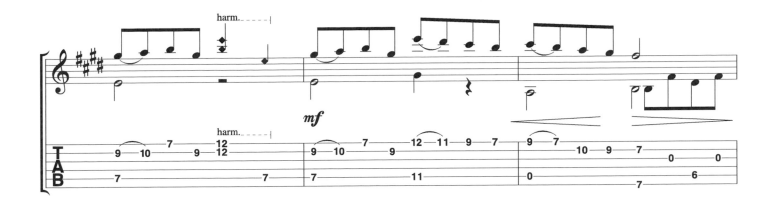

HULETH'S HEALTH

Turlough O Carolan (1670-1738)
arr. by John Loesberg

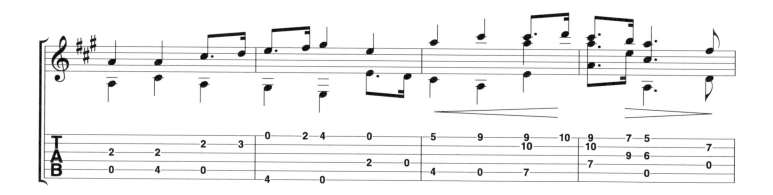

TRACK 21

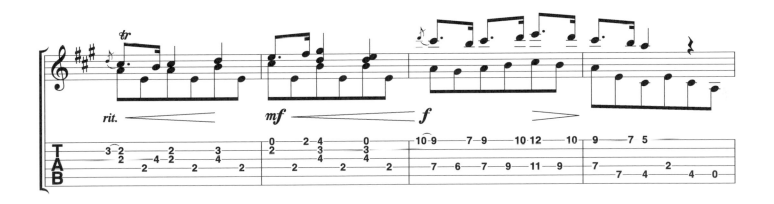

Planxty Connor

Turlough O Carolan (1670-1738)
arr. by John Loesberg

Allegretto

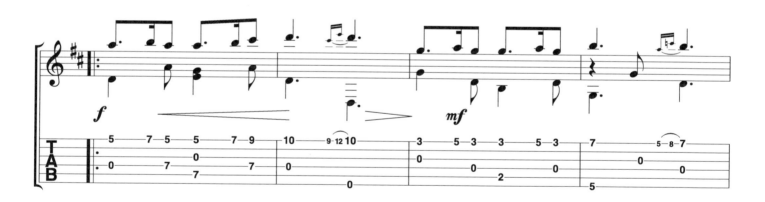

TRACK 22

Si Beag Si Mor

Turlough O Carolan (1670-1738)
arr. by John Loesberg

Andantino

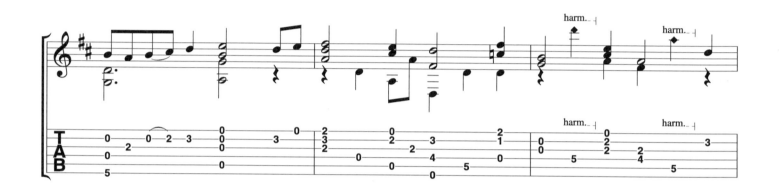

TRACK 23

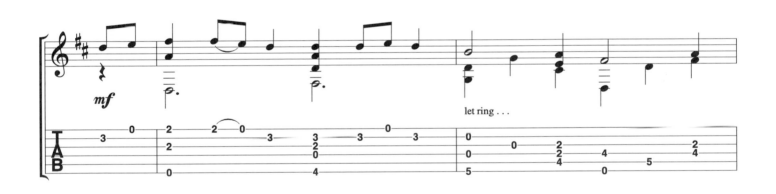

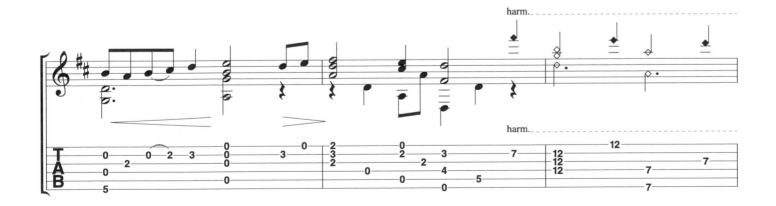

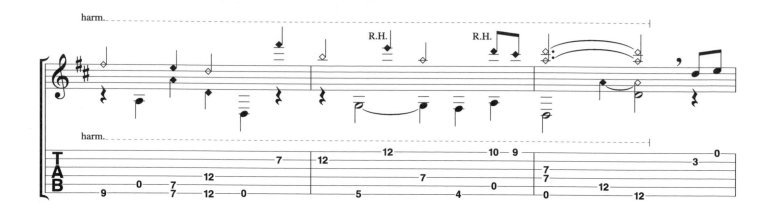
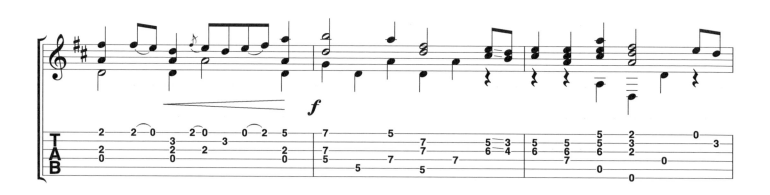
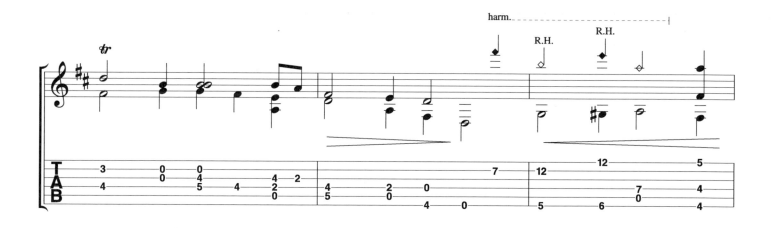
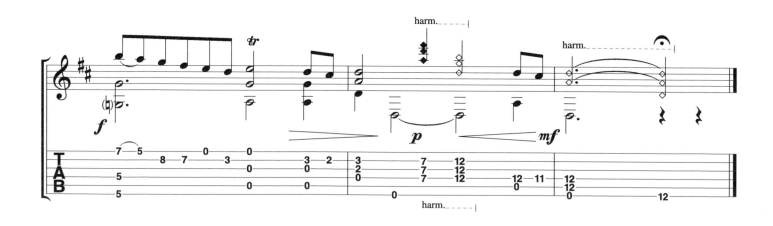

Morgan Magan

Turlough O Carolan (1670-1738)
arr. by John Loesberg

TRACK 24

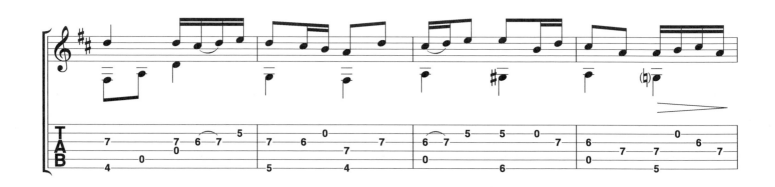

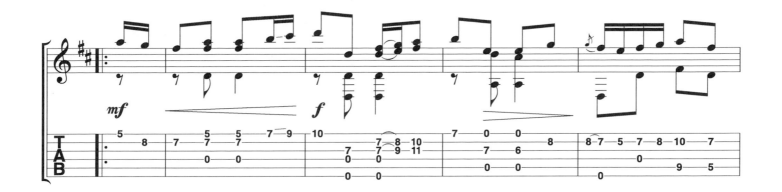

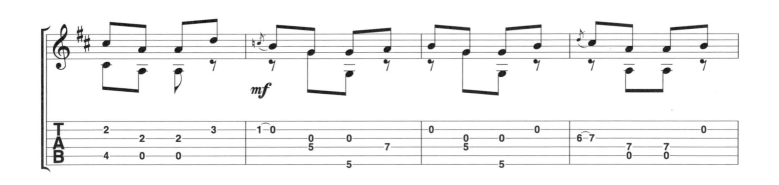

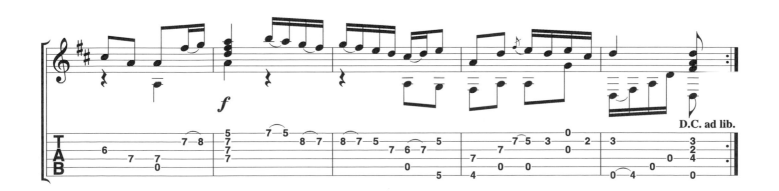

Fanny Power

Turlough O Carolan (1670-1738)
arr. by John Loesberg

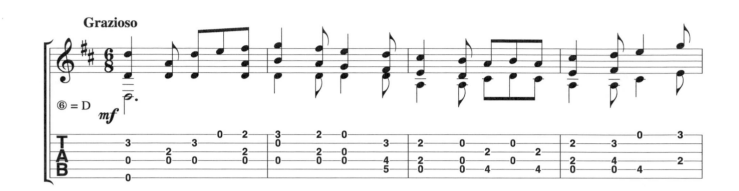

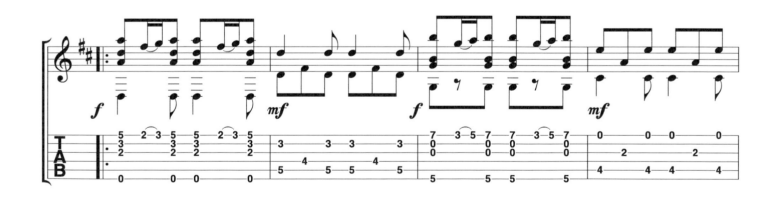

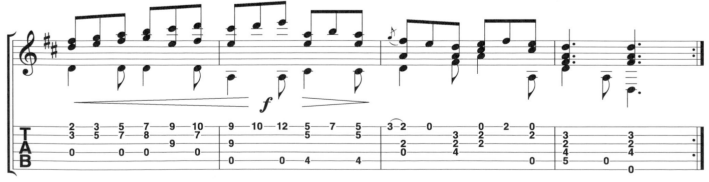

Airdí Cuan

traditional Irish
arr. by John Loesberg

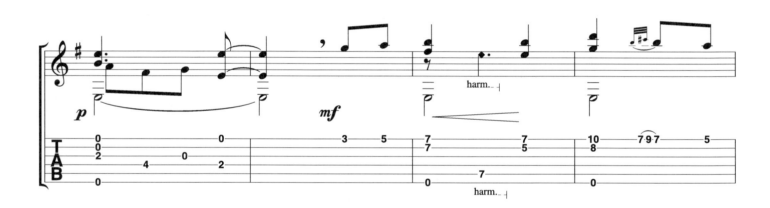

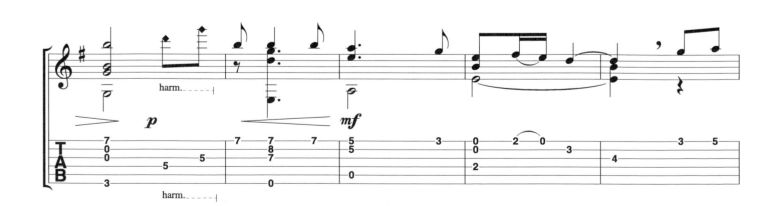

TRACK 26

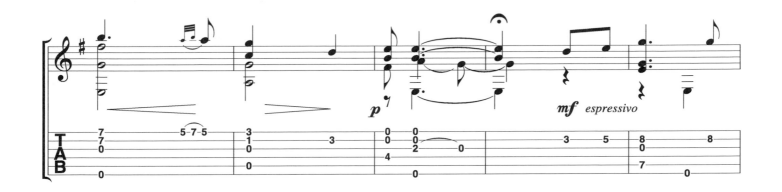

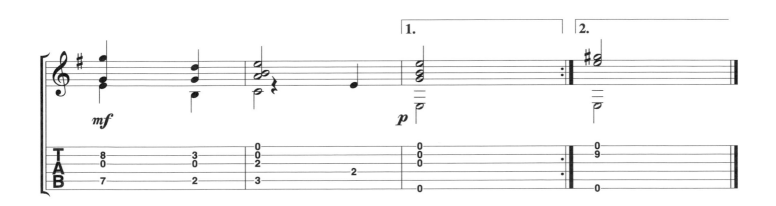

THE THREE SEACAPTAINS

traditional Irish
arr. by John Loesberg

Allegro moderato

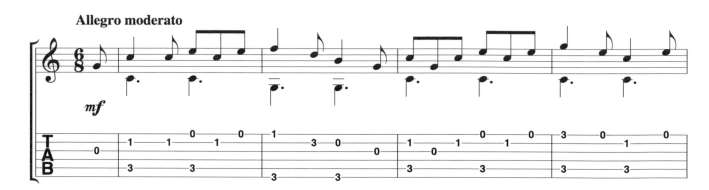

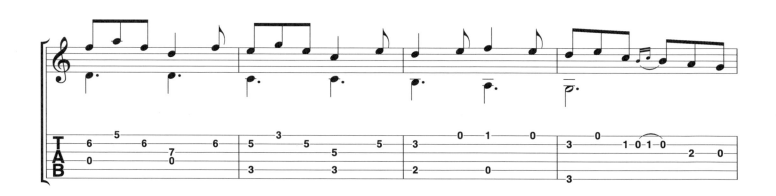

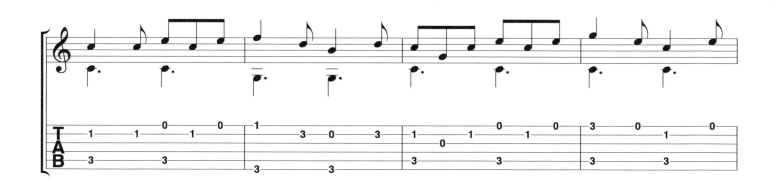

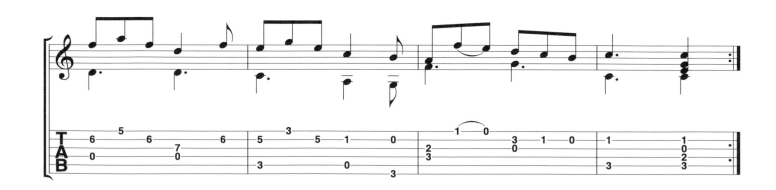

TRACK
27

Some notes on the music

The Rights of Man
This hornpipe was taken from O'Neill's great collection of Irish Traditional music 'The Dance Music of Ireland' now available in reprint from several publishers.

The Boys Of Bluehill
A lively hornpipe also taken from O'Neill's 'The Dance Music of Ireland'.

She Moved Through The Fair
Traditional Air, Words by P.J. Mac Call.
From its haunting, almost eastern sounding modal melody, this may be an air of some antiquity. The song was collected by Herbert Hughes on Co. Donegal, the words were re-written by Padraic Colum. (From 'Folksongs and Ballads Popular in Ireland' also by John Loesberg)

Baidin Fheilimi
The story of Phelim and his little boat.
A song from the North-West of the country.

Fear An Bhata
A melancholy song from Donegal which occurs in many versions throughout Scotland as well. The song tells of the plight of the wife of a boatsman lost at sea.

The Lark In The Clear Air
An ancient air, 'An tailliur.' English words by Sir Samuel Ferguson. A tune known to many in Ireland as it has been featured for years as the introduction of Ciaran Mac Mathuna's radio programme 'Mo cheol thu.' (From 'Folksongs and Ballads Popular in Ireland')

Boulavogue
One of the many scattered risings in 1798 took place in Co. Wexford under theleadership of a 'Croppy' priest, Father John Murphy. The tune is the ancient 'Youghal Harbour. (From 'Folksongs and Ballads Popular in Ireland')

Eileen Aroon
The 14th century harper Cearbhaill O'Dalaigh composed the air and wrote the original lyrics of this touching love song. The English version is by Gerald Griffin (1803-1840) better known as the author of 'The Colleen Bawn.' The full lyrics of this song may be found in Volume One of 'Folksongs and Ballads Popular In Ireland'

Did You See The Black Rogue
Taken from Bunting's 1840 Collection. This piece was notated by Bunting from the harp playing of H. Higgins in 1792. The author is unknown.

Down By The Sally Gardens
Although the words are in a poem by W. B. Yeats in a publication of 1889, a song called 'The Rambling Boys Of Pleasure' dating back to the 18th century is very much the same tune. Its first verse goes:
> It's down in the Sally's garden,
> O, there hangs rosies three.
Yeats must have found inspiration in these lines and rewrote and undoubtedly improved the original. The air is 'The Maid Of Mourne Shore.'
(From 'Folksongs and Ballads Popular In Ireland')

Spinningwheel Song
John F. Waller (1809-1894) composed this ever-popular song. The tune and rhythm really conjure up the footstirring of the girl at the wheel.
(From 'Folksongs and Ballads Popular In Ireland')

Spancil Hill
On the road between Ennis and Tulla is found the cross of Spancil Hill, where a fair is held every year at the end of July. It has the distinction of being one of the oldest horse fairs in Munster.
(From 'Folksongs and Ballads Popular In Ireland')

Carrickfergus
Named after the old town on Belfast Lough in North East Ireland. A very evocative song, parts of the lyrics can be found in the folksong repertoire of many English speaking countries. 'The Water Is Wide' is an Anglo-Scottish version which is quite well known in America.
(From 'Folksongs and Ballads Popular In Ireland')

The Irish Washerwoman

This Irish jig which, strangely enough is rather well-known abroad in orchestral arrangements but rarely played in Ireland probably because of over-familiarity. It appears in a publication by Brysson in Edinburgh. This volume was printed in 1790 and bears the title 'A curious selection of favourite tunes with variations to which is added fifty favourite Irish airs.' It contains many jigs amongst which 'The Irish Waterman' now called 'The Irish Washerwoman'. The titles of Irish traditional tunes normally have very little to do with their musical content. As a means of identifying a tune out of thousands of others, however, it is quite useful to have so many pieces with exotic names like: The Rights Of Man, Smash The Windows, The Sailor's Cravat etc.

Planxty Irwin
Carolan

Taken from the 1796 Bunting Collection. Like many of Carolan's pieces this is a song, its words are found in 'An Dunaire' by Thaddeus Connellan, 1829. This editor provides the following English translation:

We will take our way without delay.
To see a Noble, brave and gay,
The gallant Colonel near the sea,
Him I mean to treat of;
With mirth and joy he fills his glasses,
Delights to cheer both lads and lasses,
This is John I will answer,
The brave English Irelander.

This piece was for Colonel John Irwin (1680–1752) of Tanrego house on Ballisodare Bay, Co. Sligo who was high sheriff of Sligo in 1731.

Planxty Judge
Carolan

Taken from the 1809 Bunting Collection. This is a jig attached to another piece printed separately in the collection as 'Madam Judge'. Mrs Judge was the wife of Thomas Judge of Grangebeg, Co. Westmeath, whom she married in 1707.

Planxty McGuire
Carolan

The words of this song can be found in D.J. O'Sullivan's book 'Carolan the Life and Times and Music of an Irish Harper'. The song is dedicated to Constantine McGuire of Tempo, Co. Fermanagh.

The Lamentation Of Owen O Neill
Carolan

From the 1796 Bunting Collection. Owen Roe O'Neill was the commander of the Ulster army of Confederates. His death in 1649 was a national disaster and laid Ireland open to the Cromwellian settlement. This piece shows some influence of Tudor and even Elizabethan lute music and it was arranged for the guitar with this in mind.

Carolans Concerto
Carolan

Taken from the 1809 Bunting Collection. This is without doubt the best known of Carolan's works. It was dedicated to Mrs Power of Coorheen House on the shores of the lake at Loughrea, Co. Galway. Fanny Power, her daughter, had a piece dedicated to herself which is also included in this collection (Track 8d, page 50). Carolan's Concerto allegedly resulted from the rivalry between Carolan and one of the many visiting Italian musicians who often called on the Irish noblemen. The musician with whom Carolan apparently had a contest of musical skills may have been Geminiani himself.

Planxty Charles Coote
Carolan

From the 1840 Bunting Collection. Dedicated to the descendant of Sir Charles Coote, the first settler of the Coote family in Ireland. The subject of this piece may be either the 4th or 5th baronet of the same name, both of whom lived at Coote Hall, Co. Roscommon.

Huleth's Health
Carolan

From the 1809 Bunting Collection. A lively drinking song to honour a gentleman who has never been identified. In various other sources the name is spelt 'Hewlett'.

Planxty Connor
Carolan

From the 1809 Bunting Collection. Nothing much is known about the John O'Connor-Faly to whom this piece is dedicated. More than likely he was one of the O'Connors of Offaly who in Tudor times were a very powerful family. Councillor John O'Connor held the rank of Colonel in King James' army and was slain at the battle of Aughrim in 1691. It is possible that his son Maurice asked Carolan to write the piece to commemorate his father.

Sí Beag Sí Mor

Carolan

Spelt in various ways, Sí Beag Sí Mór is allegedly the first piece composed by Carolan. There is an Irish legend describing two 'fairy raths' on hilltops in Co. Leitrim, where a battle was once fought between the 'good people'. In Carolan's lyrics (in An Duanaire, T. Connellan, 1829) we are told of the great contention that arose between the two rival queens of the two Sighbrugha (fairy places). They first indulged in wordy warfare, each claiming superiority over the other. Then ensued a battle between their partisans, fought on the plain between Sí Beag and Sí Mór, "the like of which has not been seen since Troy". Finally a parley or truce is called in view of the hostile approach of the Fairy Host of two neighbouring hills, Ben Aughlin and Carn Clonhugh, and the two sides unite in the face of common danger.

Morgan Magan

Carolan

From the 1809 Bunting Collection. Composed in honour of Morgan Magan of Togherstown, Co. Westmeath, who died in 1738.

Fanny Power

Carolan

From the 1840 Bunting Collection. Fanny (Frances) Power was the daughter and heiress of David and Elizabeth Power of Coorheen, Loughrea, Co. Galway. Carolan wrote compositions for several members of the Power family. David Power (O'Sullivan No.153) and of course 'Mrs Power' (O'Sullivan No.159) which is better known as Carolan's Concerto and is also included in this volume (CD track 6b, page 35)

Airdi Cuan

An old song from the North of Ireland. Like many sean-nos songs this really could be described as a form of Irish 'Blues' with the usual many references to the passionate descriptions of troubled lives and locations.

> If I were in Airdí Cuan
> Near that mountain that's far away from me
> It would be seldom that I wouldn't go
> To the Cuckoo's Glen on a Sunday
> Chorus:
> And och, och, the whole of Ireland O
> Melancholy Ireland and O
> It's my heart is heavy and sad.
> It's many the Christmas that I was
> At the bottom of the River Doinne
> and me without sense
> Hurling on the white beach
> And my white hurley in my fist.

The Three Seacaptains

This traditional set dance is printed in O'Neill's 'The Dance Music Of Ireland' (No. 961) and various other sources.

O Carolan 1670-1738
If your appetite for the music of O Carolan has been
whetted by some of these arrangements of his work you may
want to check out
'Carolan, the Life and Times and Music of an Irish Harper'
by Donal O'Sullivan (Ossian).
This is a re-edited, complete edition of anything and
everything about O Carolan including the music of every
single composition known to exist.